EMPTY TRAINS

Sandifer-Smith

ISBN: 978-1-915079-16-9

Cover designed by Aaron Kent

Edited and typeset by Aaron Kent

Broken Sleep Books Ltd
Rhydwen,
Talgarreg,
SA44 4HB
Wales

Contents

Empty Trains

George Sandifer-Smith

For Rachael, who made it all OK – I'm so into you too

Holiday

Initially, to keep from totally losing it, I confess
to subscribing to the notion that this would be over
in three weeks; that we would drop out and use the time
to pick up new skills, bake endless loaves of cider bread
and feast on kitchen cupboard antiques. What can't you do
with a tin of chickpeas? Finally – I can do yoga. Stand
on my head after twenty-one days, the Welsh words
tumbling out like cawl from a ladle, hot splashes
peppering my poems. I saw all this. Bliss.

Eau de March

Shelves whiten empty like I've never seen
in the toiletries aisle. Unless it's for a birthday
I don't spend riches on soap. It disinfects, smells
OK, I require little more. Now all that is left

is "Hotel Style" soap. Thrice as much in
contactless payments, so perfumed
that pizza turns to lather on the tongue.
Skin cracks and creases, a micro-Martian landscape.

Crowning hour

Heavy are their heads
without equipment.

Thursday descends in Covid-time,
cloying. Hours open, shut,

like cells, unless you're beach-bound.
Sixty pounds, please. Hot sand

might burn your feet. The ventilator
might burn your throat. Your family

might burn your body. Your guest list
will be small. At 8, lean into the street

and crown them. It's brittle,
a ripple through warming

nights, a brief reign before
war resumes. In days between

each ceremony, that same coronet
is jammed on teachers' skulls

with words reserved for pubs, though
there are no pubs now.

Heavy are their heads.

I, uh, love you, Marjorie

Through the unemployed lunches
clawing at schedules
time travel is ever-present.
Yellow-stained and washed
out of their wobbling lines, voices unsettled
into the verses we know like mantras.

The product strikes us with its heart
among the frosty chocolate milkshakes,
Homer with a mouth-corner twist standing
in a pastel doorframe, lonely with a wilting bunch
of vague flowers. Generations remix this place
to draw tears, wring something a little extra even
as the Simpsons stand still, move forwards
until we are at ages with Marge and Homer.

Waimaukau

Lockdown floods both of our sleep
with revisitations as well
as shade, scar tissue on the first hour
of morning until coffee drowns it.

Last night – wasps at the window
in the kitchen, across by the living
room rising from hedges. Angry song
played on stained glass wings

battering one another, strategising
the assault on home. Stings long
as fingers carry pain, yellow and thin
black is the threat, the promise. Wake up.

Gallery, in ruins

North of Aegina overlooking
the port and welcoming, with its first
cracked view as you
approach by water – my wife stands

with her hands crossed, sunglasses
with the look of this, photograph –
a gallery frame – Apollo's temple ruins
in our flat held in black plastic,

unfinished. Like me at Sunday
carvery clean-shaven
with my mother. R and I, separate
graduations same day, same place.

Worlds occupy walls,
we inspect them
now the clock
has stopped, the map shrunk.

The Consecrations

Hard alarms for softened deadlines are one way
to halt each day in its concave way
of becoming a Sunday. Press play and dye
the morning with a recollection,
childhood home you explored in sleep, victims
we were hacked into while we kept waking
at bay. The news an instant constant required

time limits to screen-time, blue light
filters, clockwork laundry, dedicated huddling
hours for the television, measuring pieces
written in novels, poems, joke photographs of me
found covered in drawer miscellany.
Nine-to-five or near enough we built
a scaffold of routine, a way to the finish.

Jesus Christ, there wouldn't be any more packets!

In our family, we trade ancient adverts
in video form or more often posters - 'wassup',
'alright, Janice' - the stranger the
better. Lockdown and distance between
Cardiff and Carmarthen put postcards

our way. Along with boxes of Earl Grey
and sweets, a miniaturised poster for hundred
year-old Bovril. The murky brown jar destined
for Arctic exploration, back of the cupboard.
Bulls painted in red. Beef tea to winter a summer.

Watercolour

Remember that snake last summer? Paces
from the burial plot of David Lloyd George
it danced in the burning of the undisturbed
road, deaf to our feet, the cool rush of the Dwyfor
but knowing vibrations, danger. Emptier than Cardiff,

emptier than everywhere, Criccieth must be
a stillness of a paradise in Covid time. Only
the sheep, the dead, the river and that snake
grooving in the absence.

Colonise the Moon

I am not redundant, emphatically. A natural end
is what I am going through, the rope has not been cut
but simply reached its tether. Well done and remember
your mental health is important, even as you become

so much non-renewable energy. Because here I am, burnt
off like coal, choking the sky as June colours over me.
Blue. I become fossil fuel, the memory of stone knitting
a carapace of history. Dropping away into folkore, gone.

Roar Shake Roar

Behind our parking space, in slots
where tom-cats hunt, parading prey
caught in jaws on the low wall,
tracks roar a little lighter.

Empty trains or ghost trains carry dead
air in their bellies. There must be a driver
watching Wales turn into England, separate
measures dissolving. Strip lights bathe yellow

through glass that rushes on.
Empty trains still sing
and rock our mattress gently.
At least arrivals aren't delayed now.

Summer Christmas

We dug ourselves out one summer lockdown
weekend by playing at winter, uncorking cheap
fizz and delighting in the sofa, Macauley Culkin's
cruelty in setting traps of pain and
lasting damage. No presents but a full dinner,

prawn cocktail, dessert. Slabs of cheese
in different shades, veined and non-veined.
Pushing at the clock by taking the calendar off
and giving it a well-deserved spin. Blasting
the distant voice of Noddy Holder.

First snow, Stars Hollow

Lane dressed for the Lonely
Hearts Club Band, losing out
on time with Rory forcing
Fear & Loathing in Pemberley
before she's locked down too
in Hartford. Once a punk
rocker, former WWE Champ misnamed
a town near me Hartford West.

Max stays over, the first
of Lorelei's dates ever to, clearly
not long for this world. She offers
Emily an ark in jest, almost
always does she joke to a mother's
scowl. When my wife and I started
dating, we sped through this, did the dance
to the opening credits, quick quips.

Mammoth by night

Night fills natural history, even
in business hours as the gallery fears
for its visitors, doors shut,
the dust on Perseus' shield – dead skin

like realisation of the mammoth, robotic
when awakened, otherwise unplugged, button
unpressed by scared kids. It doesn't buck,
shake its wool and fiberglass trunk

and instead enjoys time with its young,
the quiet of a lack of hyenas on a loop
and whispers of school trips.
A holiday for the museum – lack of echo.

Into the harbour

Not one line – you can't rewire history so
the connections energise other lights. Different times
made different men into economy-boosting golden
citizens, not slave traders. Suck it up, that's history,
it's how to build empires, win a war, torture teenage girls
and fall at Waterloo, forever remembered in the names
of schools and streets, a seat in the hall of heroes.

A Dream of the Home Front

Bristol O2, December 2019 – what was yours?
Yes, my last was the Libertines with a hungover
friend and a late train, skipping the last song
as we struggled to not get dragged into off-faced
people shoving and sucking face.

The lads sat around the piano, Blitz-spiriting better
than the slogans we've endured since, the romance
without the lies. Pete Doherty's gone grey – who knows
if he's gone clean too? Still stylish in a riot, long-sleeved
naturally even with a hot crowd soaking, lager flying.

Santa Cruz Serenade

After Impulse Control *by Rachael Llewellyn*
Take me. To the cinema, to the scene
of the crime, either and. Meet me late
in a terrible nightclub, pass my name back
into my handbag, swap it for another.

Dress it up like suicide in memory
of cookery class with mother, cello lessons
but don't look in the case. The red door, furnace
fit to fuck with you for life. Peroxide

makes me invisible. Unless I'm working
from the warehouse, where I make it look
like an accident that sends a message.
I was a baby at the start, barely a teenager

and now, love. Refined and correct
as possible but I still need a slice,
lie in demon because Amber saw me
drop a head off a pier. Scarlet splash –

hey, I'm not here for spoilers.
Just to administrate, clean knives
and pick the glass fragments. Know
that this can't go on, waiting

for the digitalis to take hold
and the bullet to leave
the chamber. I need
my own terms to live.

Flattened

Willing the flat alive
with Radio 4, Simpsons, Gilmores,
quiet parts remain precious, only
to know they aren't quiet really –

that lone trumpet upstairs, scales last
summer, now climbing around
jazzier places, numbers to move to
and remind you: the verse, chorus, return.

Twilight marathon kit

Alcohol abounds in stretches like this,
seasons without a feast of air, summers spent
sea-free, pretending to enjoy pub quizzes
over conference call. Lost in the supermarket

wine boxes sing. Oaky, cherry, twenty-two
pounds, crisp, sharp, citrus, nineteen, and
"fruity red" - thirteen. Volume of three bottles,
hefty as Dickens and just as funny

to taste. Thin and desperate, moths soar
from my wallet and make their choice.

Dolphin legend

News spread. A whole pod came
beaking and bottling to break the green,
absence of gondolas. Venice may sink
slowly but that day, dolphins took the virus
to task. The Earth said no. People stood
in awe, blood vessels breaking their links
in their creamy eyes. Retweets began, reposts

filled the marshy foundations of
the transmissions we accept.
The infection justified – a planet holding
back its oppressors, calling no more, let
animals reign. That was the legend.

Truth thinned it down – their blue hides
were photographed in a Sardinian port
hundreds of miles away, relentlessly normally.
This breathless curse is ours and we can't benefit
from a lens pointing at the wrong churn of water.

Massive swelling organ

For Dave Greenfield (1949-2020)

When T and I were teenagers we'd press
earphones deep down flesh canals, challenge
each other to rattle small soft bones
with a Greenfield solo. How high
the arpeggios would climb, plastic ivories
tinkling like tasers. Old codgers
bringing a classical touch to leather
and snot crowds doing the dying fly
in the 100 Club, the Roundhouse, England
dreaming, sometimes screaming – no
wonder there were no more heroes.
A better rejection in its own game.

Short of a farewell tour cancelled in Covid
when a million lost their lifeblood,
Dave Greenfield played the last arpeggio, a history
in Ivor Novellos and Golden Brown. A gentle heart,
a rat farm, an unfinished pint. "He was
the difference between the Stranglers
and every other punk band."

Platform One

Veins of white move through black pillars,
marble at the Seren Poetry Festival 2020.
I watched the sun consume the Earth
here, I saw daemons scatter the floor
as explorers traversed the Arctic on paper
for a city written in Dust here.
James Dean Bradfield opens up
about *Clueless Dogs* and "bass! How low
can you go?" - boxes of books passed
down by the dead of Blackwood.

That was the last big one for me, soggy trainers
and fair coffee in Cardiff's Temple of Peace built
on the heavy absent air of trenches. Poets gather,
weddings and worship. All slips to sheets of plastic
where we meet now. Swap verses and convert
the many rooms of the Temple into our study,
watching the battery life, the faces switching order
depending on how voices carry through the static.

A Murigen path opens

The river, beside the trainlines
where speakers say 'this is a staff announcement'
before garbling the rest of their verse, has grown
important in persistent times, memory.
We spend our outdoor exercise hour mapping
a square route angling back to a fence
we can see the river through, murking beside
released traffic, rare cars
delivering medication or pizza.

The Rhymney River and Afon Rhymni begins
its day, should rivers wish to measure themselves
in hours and seconds like ours, passing glacial down
to draw lines between Glamorgan and Monmouthshire
until Victorian parishes were rendered
in the Cardiff afterlife, running a capital
towards the Severn Estuary. Cold water clarifies

and is neither Welsh nor English. We listen,
a formerly-black body cleansed in the death
of choking, dusty industries that fed a world.
We don't see the trout now clearing
the distance to the upper reaches.

Gwynneth

"I didn't realise Wales wasn't in England...Fuck you Wales you bunch of bastards."

Police approach in Barmouth, across sands
that will absolve your footprints
with a little help from ocean water that soaks
boundaries and blurs, in these soft patches.

Today, the mercury overflows and quicksilvers
judgement, maybe. Or it's just a non-understanding
of devolution – how voices share crusts of dirt
but alter in the hard heat of summer 2020.

You call on B___s when laws break, invoke
his name like a mate down the pub, spell-
casting open the trap. Nobody has Karenned
like you have today, against a nation of dragons.

Receivers

You and I have never been as digital
as these months have coded us.
Friends have slipped their flesh
into lines of light, short verse. Worse,
the ones already made of numbers
and blue walls, feeds pumping as arteries
cataloguing as they caterwaul into
spools of tape imagined but cooled
in deserts and other uninhabitable spaces,

solidify themselves and make addicts
of us. Wars begin with characters
of two-hundred and eighty, and characters
from television begin wars, and conjurers strip
their goodwill away from the castles they built,
the birthday parties they filled and worst stories
they gave us. The glass on them fogs, our desires
lost. The world entire fills our iPhone screens,
receive it in transmission, translation, crushed
down its hateful components, diet plans.

Deadline

We cheat, sort of. Use a sack of rice
to minimise crowd contact for a friend.

In doing so, we hang out. Park up,
wave across the tarmac, painted spaces

borders now. A cup of tea would push it
but we've brought our own pop. Noting

the feet between us, they back away,
I stroll into car park no man's land

and place the rice and forgotten tupperware
like hostages. Turn back and walk

as if we are duelling. A month before
we'd sat in crowded pubs, as close

as you are to this page.

Scranton

Pennsylvanian town that folds into a box
we keep in the bedroom, beside the VHS built-in
television my wife's had since childhood.
We circle this Slough comparable, round

and round as it grows and loses its lead,
return to reception. Repeating each story:
the beet farmer and the uptight accountant,
the Michael Scott Paper Company, the births

of babies rushed through the office. Laughing
to hold the building together
and keep the walls of our flat
international, filled with a future.

First Saturday back in August

In the Bay and the centre, all places inbetween
where lager foams and gin dances with tonic bubbles,

in numbers written as decent in the article with pavements
possibly choked but only as much as is sexy,

in bank accounts which fall away into empty space
while rumours start that it's a myth, the hospitals empty,

in your glass on the first Saturday back find the alarm.
It hasn't gone off yet. There is no cure.

Get hard

Welsh law doesn't touch the masks and August
on forgets the death count. Supermarkets fall
into the first excursion, looking strangely
at you as your glasses fog a little, hot air rising
from the cloth on your nostrils. Later – deaths

keeping up – movements start. Presidents elsewhere
play wounded, the looks stop being strange.
Now lips curl. Eyes turn hungry, angry – the masks
are sent to control us by a communist cabal.
You become part of the problem by partaking

in safety measures. Bare-faced blokes,
tight t-shirts, older – they veer nearer than two metres
to tell you in swinging arms, jackboot footsteps
that you deserve to lose everything, funnily enough
like ones fleeing from war-torn states – "educate yourself."

The Greatest Comeback in the History of Sport

Horses are the first to be run
for our pleasure and economy.

Silent stadiums sound
like PE lessons, wet turf, boot.

That the Crucible could sound more
like a late night should be impossible.

Betting shops bombard my channels, promise
the greatest comeback is sport itself.

Forest school

At least my children can learn
with leaves beneath their feet,
luckily close behind the house.
Fractions first, then we identify
trees which are like people, different.

After lunch we take the guitars
and simple chords unfold with birds
that chorus. Lockdown is accompanied
here, without a future yet. The raving
and rioting waits at the starting line

and I can know that for now, my children
will be safe from the maskless masses
that haven't gathered like deeply-bruised
clouds quickly on a golden day. One moment
early in the ordeal – for them, I'll take it.

Green Chorus

Carmarthen
Pulling beans from their ascent
to butter. The same blackbird two days
in a row on the converted outhouse relic
leads the chorus as laws soften gingerly.

Nuneaton
Fat horned caterpillar dances red-brown
fence freshened by family, new furniture,
rare crisps. Barbeque melody spits to split
verses, into the chorus. Laws soften but solidify.

Acknowledgements

I am indebted to Aaron Kent and the team at Broken Sleep for giving this pamphlet a chance and working on it with me – it's so exciting to join so many of my literary heroes on the roster of one of the UK's most excellent publishers.

The poem 'A Murigen path opens' was first published under an alternative title in *Ayaskala Magazine* in Autumn 2020, and the poems 'I, uh, love you, Marjorie' and 'Santa Cruz Serenade' were first aired on Damien Donnelly's poetry podcast *Eat The Storms*.

Thanks also to my family, Joy, Ian, and Mili, and my in-laws Lesley, Paul, Ieuan, Charlotte, and Andy, for keeping us (relatively) stable during the first lockdown that this book covers. I particularly thank my then-fiancee Rachael, now my wife, for keeping it together and encouraging me to process the pandemic in a healthy poetic manner. She's the best.

LAY OUT YOUR UNREST

www.ingramcontent.com/pod-product-compliance
Lightning Source LLC
Chambersburg PA
CBHW030622070426
42448CB00045B/1248